HOOVES AND CLAWS

Jason Cooper

Rourke
Publishing LLC
Vero Beach, Florida 32964

www.rourkepublishing.com

PHOTO CREDITS: All photos © Lynn M. Stone

Title page: A bear uses claws for defense.

Editor: Robert Stengard-Olliges

Cover design by Nicola Stratford.

Library of Congress Cataloging-in-Publication Data

Cooper, Jason.
  Hooves and claws / Jason Cooper.
      p. cm. — (Let's look at animals)
  Includes index.
  ISBN 1-60044-173-4 (Hardcover)
  ISBN 1-59515-526-0 (Softcover)
  1. Hoofs—Juvenile literature. 2. Claws—Juvenile literature. I. Title.
II. Series: Cooper, Jason. Let's look at animals.
  QL942.S74 2007
  591.47'9—dc22
                                2006012633

Printed in the USA

CG/CG

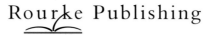

Rourke Publishing

www.rourkepublishing.com – sales@rourkepublishing.com
Post Office Box 3328, Vero Beach, FL 32964

Table of Contents

Hooves

Animals have many different kinds of feet. Some **four-legged** animals have hooves on their feet.

Hooves cover the animal's feet and toes. Hooves are like four hard shoes. Hooves grow from skin. They become hard, though, like horns.

Most hooved animals walk or run a lot. Their hooves help protect their feet. Hooves also help animal feet grip soil or rock.

Hooves are shaped for special uses. Horse hooves are for running.

Many Animals Have Hooves

Farm animals with hooves are sheep, goats, and cattle. Horses, donkeys, mules, and pigs have hooves, too.

Many wild animals have hooves. Some are zebras, deer, peccaries, hippos, camels, giraffes, antelopes, bison, and **rhinos**.

How Many Toes?

Some hooved animals have an odd number of toes.
The horse, for example, has one toe inside its hooves.
Other animals, like cattle, have an even number of toes.

Bighorn sheep have two toes on each hoof. Two toes help the sheep climb mountains.

Claws

Many kinds of four-legged animals have claws instead of hooves. Hooves are blunt. Claws are sharp. Claws grow from the end of toes.

An animal's claws match how it lives. Raccoon claws are for climbing. Claws may be short and straight.

The heavy claws of **marmots** and badgers are for digging. They may be long and curved.

Claws are Sharp

Bears climb, fight, and dig with their long claws.

The claws of wild cats usually stay hidden in their paws. Hidden claws stay sharp.

But cats can push their claws out. Cats use their claws to help hold and tear **prey.**

Claws for Eating

Claws catch, hold, and tear. Claws help grab and rip prey into bite-size pieces. The bear's claws help turn a slippery fish into dinner.

Owls, hawks, and eagles use their claws to kill and carry prey. The claws of these hunting birds are called **talons**.

Glossary

four-legged (FOR LEG ed) — to have four legs, like a horse or dog

marmot (MAR mit) — a kind of woodchuck; a large ground squirrel of the West

prey (PRAY) — an animal that is food for another animal

rhino (RHINE o) — nickname for rhinoceros

talons (TAL uhnz) — the sharp claws of hawks, owls, and eagles

Index

FURTHER READING

Hall, Peg and Dulap, Julie. *Whose Feet Are These?* Picture Window Books, 2002.

Goodman, Susan E. *Claws, Coats, and Camouflage.* Lerner, 2001.

WEBSITES TO VISIT

http://en.wikipedia.org/wiki/Claw

http://animal.discovery.com/guides/cats/body/clawsintro.html

ABOUT THE AUTHOR

Jason Cooper has written many children's books for Rourke Publishing about a variety of topics. Cooper travels widely to gather information for his books.